ON THE

DEITY OF JESUS OF NAZARETH

AN ENQUIRY
INTO THE NATURE OF JESUS
BY AN EXAMINATION OF THE SYNOPTIC GOSPELS.

BY

THE WIFE OF A BENEFICED CLERGYMAN

EDITED AND PREFACED BY

REV. CHARLES VOYSEY, B.A.

PUBLISHED BY THOMAS SCOTT,
NO. 11 THE TERRACE, FARQUHAR ROAD, UPPER NORWOOD,
LONDON, S.E.

1873.

In the interest of creating a more extensive selection of rare historical book reprints, we have chosen to reproduce this title even though it may possibly have occasional imperfections such as missing and blurred pages, missing text, poor pictures, markings, dark backgrounds and other reproduction issues beyond our control. Because this work is culturally important, we have made it available as a part of our commitment to protecting, preserving and promoting the world's literature. Thank you for your understanding.

EDITOR'S PREFACE.

THE following pages were put into my hands by a lady—the wife of a beneficed clergyman. Not wishing to compromise her husband, she has withheld her name from publication, and deserves all honour for the concession. But the fact led me to write a few words as a Preface, in which I would remind the Bishops and dignitaries of our Church that this is no uncommon case. Orthodoxy is riddled through and through with heresy. Every family has its heretic. And although but few clergymen or their wives could be found to write such an Essay as the following with equally felicitous logic and simplicity, there are many quite capable of relishing arguments so lucidly stated and so ably drawn. If most of Mr Scott's regular readers are familiar with the line of argument, there are many outside the circle whom this pamphlet may reach to whom it will be new, and whom it may powerfully affect.

The position which the person of Jesus occupies in modern Christendom is the very citadel of Christianity, and on the settlement of his claims will turn the future of the Churches.

We, who have been all our lives sceptics, are growing weary of the very name; but we must not forget that we have a great duty to perform towards those who are yet orthodox, or are clinging, like some Unitarians, to the skirts of a fading system.

When I first knew this lady, she had given up all points of disputed orthodoxy except this one of the nature of Jesus, whom she still regarded as perfect and divine. Careful and independent study of the whole question, however, led her at length to see the facts clearly—to own them to herself in spite of strong predilections the other way—and to write them down here for the benefit of others.

In the course of this change I was appealed to for an authoritative opinion. I absolutely refused to give one. I refused to be made the means of shovelling second-hand opinions into any one's mind. All I said was—"If you believe Christ to be God, stick to it: you are not obliged to believe as I do. Only make up your mind for yourself." This was no case of converting or proselytising. It was one of independent growth and natural conviction.

There are hundreds of clergymen, and clergymen's wives too, who are fast treading the same road, if they have not yet reached the same goal.

The alarmists are quite right. *Christianity is in terrible danger.* We wish we could add—*in extremis;* but when the break up of a faith has begun with its teachers, with those most interested in its being maintained, the days of that faith are numbered.

Such little works as this Essay, if well placed and well digested, will do more to open people's eyes than many a more pretentious and elaborate treatise.

CHARLES VOYSEY.

Camden House, Dulwich, S.E., March, 1873.

ON THE
DEITY OF JESUS OF NAZARETH.

"WHAT think ye of Christ, whose son is he?" Human child of human parents, or divine Son of the Almighty God? When we consider his purity, his faith in the Father, his forgiving patience, his devoted work among the offscourings of society, his brotherly love to sinners and outcasts—when our minds dwell on these alone, we all feel the marvellous fascination which has drawn millions to the feet of this "son of man," and the needle of our faith begins to tremble towards the Christian pole. If we would keep unsullied the purity of our faith in God alone, we are obliged to turn our eyes sometimes—however unwillingly—towards the other side of the picture and to mark the human weaknesses which remind us that he is but one of our race. His harshness to his mother, his bitterness towards some of his opponents, the marked failure of one or two of his rare prophecies, the palpable limitation of his knowledge—little enough, indeed, when all are told,—are more than enough to show us that, however great as man, he is not the All-righteous, the All-seeing, the All-knowing, God.

No one, however, whom Christian exaggeration has not goaded into unfair detraction, or who is not blinded by theological hostility, can fail to revere portions of the character sketched out in the three synoptic gospels. I shall not dwell here on the Christ of the fourth Evangelist: we can scarcely trace in that figure the lineaments of the Jesus of Nazareth whom we have learnt to love.

I propose, in this essay, to examine the claims of Jesus to be more than the man he appeared to be during his life-time: claims—be it noted—which are put forward on his behalf by others rather than by himself. His own assertions of his divinity are to be found only in the unreliable fourth gospel, and in it they are destroyed by the sentence there put into his mouth with strange inconsistency: "If I bear witness of myself, my witness is not true."

It is evident that by his contemporaries Jesus was not regarded as God incarnate. The people in general appear to have looked upon him as a great prophet, and to have often debated among themselves whether he were their expected Messiah or not. The band of men who accepted him as their teacher were as far from worshipping him as God as were their fellow-countrymen: their prompt desertion of him when attacked by his enemies, their complete hopelessness when they saw him overcome and put to death, are sufficient proofs that though they regarded him—to quote their own words—as "a prophet mighty in word and deed," they never guessed that the teacher they followed, and the friend they lived with in the intimacy of social life, was Almighty God Himself. As has been well pointed out, if they believed their Master to be God, surely when they were attacked they would have fled to him for protection, instead of endeavouring to save themselves by deserting him: we may add that this would have been their natural instinct, since they could never have imagined beforehand that the Creator Himself could really be taken captive by His creatures and suffer death at their hands. The third class of his contemporaries, the learned Pharisees and Scribes, were as far from regarding him as divine as were the people or his disciples. They seem to have viewed the new teacher somewhat contemptuously at first, as one who unwisely persisted in expounding the highest doctrines to the many, instead of—a second Hillel—adding to the stores of their own learned circle. As his influence spread and appeared to be undermining their own,—still more, when he placed himself in direct opposition, warning the people against them,—they were roused to a course of active hostility, and at length determined to save themselves by destroying him. But all through their passive contempt and direct antagonism, there is never a trace of their dreaming him to be anything more than a religious enthusiast who finally became dangerous: we never for a moment see them assuming the manifestly absurd position, of men knowingly measuring their strength against God, and endeavouring to silence and destroy their Maker. So much for the opinions of those who had the best opportunities of observing his ordinary life. A "good man," a "deceiver," a "mighty prophet," such are the recorded opinions of his contemporaries: not one is found to step forward and proclaim him to be Jehovah, the God of Israel.

One of the most trusted strongholds of Christians, in defending their Lord's Divinity, is the evidence of prophecy. They gather from the sacred books of the Jewish nation the predictions of the longed-for Messiah, and claim them as prophecies fulfilled in Jesus of Nazareth. But there is one stubborn fact which destroys the force of this argument: the Jews, to whom these writings belong, and who from tradition and national peculiarities, may reasonably be supposed to be the best exponents of their own prophets, emphatically deny that these prophecies are fulfilled in Jesus at all. Indeed, one main reason for their rejection of Jesus is precisely this, that he does not resemble in any way the predicted Messiah. There is no doubt that the Jewish nation were eagerly looking for their Deliverer when Jesus was born; these very longings produced several pseudo-Messiahs, who each gained in turn a considerable following, because each bore some resemblance to the expected Prince. Much of the popular rage which swept Jesus to his death was the re-action of disappointment after the hopes raised by the position of authority he assumed. The sudden burst of anger against one so benevolent and inoffensive can only be explained by the intense hopes excited by his regal entry into Jerusalem, and the utter destruction of those hopes by his failing to ascend the throne of David. Proclaimed as David's son, he came riding on an ass as king of Zion, and allowed himself to be welcomed as the king of Israel: there his short fulfilling of the prophecies ended, and the people, furious at his failing them, rose and clamoured for his death. Because he did *not* fulfil the ancient Jewish oracles, he died: he was too noble for the *rôle* laid down in them for the Messiah, his ideal was far other than that of a conqueror, with "garments rolled in blood." But even if, against all evidence, Jesus was one with the Messiah of the prophets, this would destroy, instead of implying, his Divine claims. For the Jews were pure monotheists; their Messiah was a prince of David's line, the favoured servant, the anointed of Jehovah, the king who should rule in His name: a Jew would shrink with horror from the blasphemy of seating Messiah on Jehovah's throne, remembering how their prophets had taught them that their God "would not give His honour to another." So that, as to prophecy, the case stands thus: If Jesus be the Messiah prophesied of in the old Jewish books, then he is not God: if he be not the Messiah, Jewish prophecy is silent as regards him altogether, and an appeal to prophecy is absolutely useless.

After the evidence of prophecy Christians generally rely on that furnished by miracles. It is remarkable that Jesus himself laid but little stress on his miracles; in fact, he refused to appeal to them as credentials of his authority, and either could not or would not work them when met with determined unbelief. We must notice also that the people, while "glorifying God, who had given such power unto *men*," were not inclined to admit his miracles as proofs of his right to claim absolute obedience: his miracles did not even invest him with such sacredness as to protect him from arrest and death. Herod, on his trial, was simply anxious to see him work a miracle, as a matter of curiosity. This stolid indifference to marvels as attestations of authority, is natural enough, when we remember that Jewish history was crowded with miracles, wrought for and against the favoured people, and also that they had been specially warned against being misled by signs and wonders. Without entering into the question whether miracles are possible, let us, for argument's sake, take them for granted, and see what they are worth as proofs of Divinity. If Jesus fed a multitude with a few loaves, so did Elisha: if he raised the dead, so did Elijah and Elisha; if he healed lepers, so did Moses and Elisha; if he opened the eyes of the blind, Elisha smote a whole army with blindness and afterward restored their sight: if he cast out devils, his contemporaries, by his own testimony, did the same. If miracles prove Deity, what miracle of Jesus can stand comparison with the divided Red Sea of Moses, the stoppage of the earth's motion by Joshua, the check of the rushing waters of the Jordan by Elijah's cloak? If we are told that these men worked by *conferred* power and Jesus by *inherent*, we can only answer that this is a gratuitous assumption and begs the whole question. The Bible records the miracles in equivalent terms: no difference is drawn between the manner of working of Elisha or Jesus; of each it is sometimes said they prayed; of each it is sometimes said they spake. Miracles indeed must not be relied on as proofs of divinity, unless believers in them are prepared to pay divine honours not to Jesus only, but also to a crowd of others, and to build a Christian Pantheon to the new found gods.

So far we have only seen the insufficiency of the usual Christian arguments to establish a doctrine so stupendous and so *primâ facie* improbable, as the incarnation of the Divine Being: this kind of negative testimony, this insufficient evidence, is not however the principal reason which compels Theists to protest against the central dogma of Christianity. The stronger proofs of the simple manhood of Jesus remain, and we now proceed to positive evidence of his not being God. I propose to draw attention to the traces of human infirmity in his noble character, to his absolute mistakes in prophecy, and to his evidently limited knowledge. In accepting as substantially true the account of Jesus given by the evangelists, we are taking his character as it appeared to his devoted followers. We have not to do with slight blemishes, inserted by envious detractors of his greatness; the history of Jesus was written when his disciples worshipped him as God, and his manhood, in their eyes, reached ideal perfection. We are then forced to believe that, in the Gospels, the life of Jesus is given at its highest, and that he was, at least, not more spotless than he appears in these records of his friends. But here again, in order not to do a gross injustice, we must put aside the fourth Gospel: to study his character "according to S. John" would need a separate essay, so different is it from that drawn by the three; and by all rules of history we should judge him by the earlier records, more especially as they corroborate each other in the main.

The first thing which jars upon an attentive reader of the Gospels is the want of affection and respect shown by Jesus to his mother. When only a child of twelve he lets his parents leave Jerusalem to return home, while he repairs alone to the temple. The fascination of the ancient city and the gorgeous temple services was doubtless almost overpowering to a thoughtful Jewish boy, more especially on his first visit: but the careless forgetfulness of his parents' anxiety must be considered as a grave childish fault, the more so as its character is darkened by the indifference shown by his answer to his mother's grieved reproof. That no high, though mistaken, sense of duty kept him in Jerusalem is evident from his return home with his parents; for had he felt that "his Father's business" detained him in Jerusalem at all, it is evident that this sense of duty would not have been satisfied by a three days' delay. But the Christian advocate would bar criticism by an appeal to the Deity of Jesus: he asks us therefore to believe, that Jesus, being God, saw with indifference his parents' anguish at discovering his absence; knew all about that three-days' agonised search (for they, ignorant of his divinity, felt the terrible anxiety as to his safety, natural to country people losing a child in a crowded city); did not, in spite of the tremendous powers at his command, take any steps to re-assure them; and, finally, met them again with no words of sympathy, only with a mysterious allusion, incomprehensible to them, to some higher claim than theirs, which, however, he promptly set aside to obey them. If God was incarnate in a boy, we may trust that example as a model of childhood: yet, are Christians prepared to set this "early piety and desire for religious instruction" before their young children as an example they are to follow? Are boys and girls of twelve to be free to absent themselves for days from their parents' guardianship under the plea that a higher business claims their attention? This episode of the childhood of Jesus should be relegated to those "gospels of the infancy" full of most unchildlike acts, which the wise discretion of Christendom has stamped with disapproval. The same want of filial reverence appears later in his life: on one occasion he was teaching, and his mother sent in, desiring to speak to him: the sole reply recorded to the message is the harsh remark: "Who is my mother?" The most practical proof that Christian morality has, on this head, outstripped the example of Jesus, is the prompt disapproval which similar conduct would meet with in the present day. By the strange warping of morality often caused by controversial exigencies, this want of filial reverence has been triumphantly pointed out by Christian divines; the indifference shown by Jesus to family ties is accepted as a proof that he was more than man! Thus, conduct which they implicitly acknowledge to be unseemly in a son to his mother, they claim as natural and right in the Son of God, to His! In the present day if a person is driven by conscience to a course painful to those who have claims on his respect, his recognised duty, as well as his natural instinct, is to try and make up by added affection and more courteous deference for the pain he is forced to inflict: above all, he would not wantonly add to that pain by public and uncalled-for disrespect.

The attitude of Jesus towards his opponents in high places was marked with unwarrantable bitterness. Here also the lofty and gentle spirit of his whole life has moulded Christian opinion in favour of a course different on this head to his own, so that abuse of an opponent is now commonly called *un*-Christian. Wearied with three years' calumny and contempt, sore at the little apparent success which rewarded his labour, full of a sad foreboding that his enemies would shortly crush him, Jesus was goaded into passionate denunciations: "Woe unto you, Scribes and Pharisees, hypocrites ... ye fools and blind ... ye make a proselyte twofold more the child of hell than yourselves ... ye serpents, ye generation of vipers, how can ye escape the damnation of hell!" Surely this is not the spirit which breathed in, "If ye love them which love you, what thanks have ye? ... Love your enemies, bless them that curse you, pray for them that persecute you." Had he not even specially forbidden the very expression, "Thou fool!" Was not this rendering "evil for evil, railing for railing?"

It is painful to point out these blemishes: reverence for the great leaders of humanity is a duty dear to all human hearts; but when homage turns into idolatry, then men must rise up to point out faults which otherwise they would pass over in respectful silence, mindful only of the work so nobly done.

I turn then, with a sense of glad relief, to the evidence of the limited knowledge of Jesus, for here no blame attaches to him, although *one* proved mistake is fatal to belief in his Godhead. First as to prophecy: "The Son of man shall come in the glory of his Father with his angels: and then shall he reward every man according to his works. Verily I say unto you, There be some standing here which shall not taste of death till they see the Son of man coming in his kingdom." Later, he amplifies the same idea: he speaks of a coming tribulation, succeeded by his own return, and then adds the emphatic declaration: "Verily I say unto you, This generation shall not pass till all these things be done." The non-fulfilment of these prophecies is simply a question of fact: let men explain away the words now as they may, yet, if the record is true, Jesus did believe in his own speedy return, and impressed the same belief on his followers. It is plain, indeed, that he succeeded in impressing it on them, from the references to his return scattered through the epistles. The latest writings show an anxiety to remove the doubts which were disturbing the converts consequent on the non-appearance of Jesus, and the fourth Gospel omits any reference to his coming. It is worth remarking in the latter, the spiritual sense which is hinted at—either purposely or unintentionally—in the words, "The hour . . . now is when the dead shall hear the voice of the Son of God, they that hear shall live." These words may be the popular feeling on the advent and resurrection, forced on the Christians by the failure of their Lord's prophecies in any literal sense. He could not be mistaken, *ergo* they must spiritualise his words. The limited knowledge of Jesus is further evident from his confusing Zacharias the son of Jehoiada with Zacharias the son of Barachias: the former, a priest, was slain in the temple court, as Jesus states; but the son of Barachias was Zacharias, or Zechariah, the prophet.* He himself owned a limitation of his knowledge, when he confessed his ignorance of the day of his own return, and said it was known to the "Father only." Of the same class of sayings is his answer to the mother of James and John, that the high seats of the coming kingdom "are not mine to give." That Jesus believed in the fearful doctrine of eternal punishment is evident, in spite of the ingenious attempts to prove that the doctrine is not scriptural: that he, in common with his countrymen, ascribed many diseases to the immediate power of Satan, which we should now probably refer to natural causes, as epilepsy, mania, and the like, is also self-evident. But on such points as these it is useless to dwell, for the Christian believes them on the authority of Jesus, and the subjects, from their nature, cannot be brought to the test of ascertained facts. Of the same character are some of his sayings: his discouraging "Strive to enter in at the strait gate, *for* many," etc.; his using in defence of partiality Isaiah's awful prophecy, "that seeing they may see and not perceive," etc.; his using Scripture at one time as binding, while he, at another, depreciates it; his fondness for silencing an opponent by an ingenious retort: all these things are blameworthy to those who regard him as man, while they are

* See Appendix, page 20.

shielded from criticism by his divinity to those who worship him as God. Their morality is a question of opinion, and it is wasted time to dwell on them when arguing with Christians, whose moral sense is for the time held in check by their mental prostration at his feet. But the truth of the quoted prophecies, and the historical fact of the parentage of Zachariah, can be tested, and on these Jesus made palpable mistakes. The obvious corollary is, that being mistaken—as he was—his knowledge was limited, and was therefore human, not divine.

In turning to the teaching of Jesus (I still confine myself to the three Gospels), we find no support of the Christian theory. If we take his didactic teaching, we can discover no trace of his offering himself as an object of either faith or worship. His life's work, as teacher, was to speak of the Father. In the sermon on the Mount he is always striking the keynote, "your heavenly Father;" in teaching his disciples to pray, it is to "Our Father," and the Christian idea of ending a prayer "through Jesus Christ" is quite foreign to the simple filial spirit of their master. Indeed, when we think of the position Jesus holds in Christian theology, it seems strange to notice the utter absence of any suggestion of duty to himself throughout this whole code of so-called Christian morality. In strict accordance with his more formal teaching is his treatment of inquirers: when a young man comes kneeling, and, addressing him as "Good Master," asks what he shall do to inherit eternal life, the loyal heart of Jesus first rejects the homage, before he proceeds to answer the all-important question: "Why callest thou *me* good : there is none good but one, that is, God." He then directs the youth on the way to eternal life, and *he sends that young man home without one word of the doctrine on which, according to Christians, his salvation rested.* If the "Gospel" came to that man later, he would reject it on the authority of Jesus who had told him a different "way of salvation;" and if Christianity is true, the perdition of that young man's soul is owing to the defective teaching of Jesus himself. Another time, he tells a Scribe that the first commandment is that God is one, and that all a man's love is due to Him; then adding the duty of neighbourly love, he says; "There is *none other* commandment greater than these:" so that belief in Jesus, if incumbent at all, must come after love to God and man, and is not necessary, by his own testimony, to "entering into life." On Jesus himself then rests the primary responsibility of affirming that belief in him is a matter of secondary importance, at most, letting alone the fact that he never inculcated belief in his Deity as an article of faith at all. In the same spirit of frank loyalty to God, are his words on the unpardonable sin: in answer to a gross personal affront, he tells his insulters that they shall be forgiven for speaking against him, a simple son of man, but warns them of the danger of confounding the work of God's Spirit with that of Satan, "because they said" that works done by God, using Jesus as His instrument, were done by Beelzebub.

There remains yet one argument of tremendous force, which can only be appreciated by personal meditation. We find Jesus praying to God, relying on God, in his greatest need crying in agony to God for deliverance, in his last struggle, deserted by his friends, asking why God, his God, had also forsaken him. We feel how natural, how true to life, this whole account is: in our heart's reverence for that noble life, that "faithfulness unto death," we can scarcely bear to think of the insult offered to it by Christian lips: they take every beauty out of it by telling us that through all that struggle Jesus was the Eternal, the Almighty, God: it is all apparent, not real: in his temptation he could not fall: in his prayers he needed no support: in his cry that the cup might pass away he foresaw it was inevitable: in his agony of desertion and loneliness he was present everywhere with God. In all that life, then, there is no hope for man, no pledge of man's victory, no promise for humanity. This is no *man's* life at all, it is only a wonderful drama enacted on earth. What God could do is no measure of man's powers: what have we in common with this " God-man ?" This Jesus, whom we had thought our brother, is, after all, removed from us by the immeasurable distance which separates the feebleness of man from the omnipotence of God. Nothing can compensate us for such a loss as this. We had rejoiced in that many-sided nobleness, and its very blemishes were dear, because they assured us of his brotherhood to ourselves: we are given an ideal picture where we had studied a history, another Deity where we had hoped to emulate a life. Instead of the encouragement we had found, what does Christianity offer us ?—a perfect life ? But we knew before that God was perfect: an example ? it starts from a different level: a Saviour ? we cannot be safer than we are with God: an Advocate ? we need none with our Father: a Substitute to endure God's wrath for us ? we had rather trust God's justice to punish us as we deserve, and His wisdom to do what is best for us. As God, Jesus can give us nothing that we have not already in his Father and ours: as man, he gives us all the encouragement and support which we derive from every noble soul which God sends into this world, " a burning and a shining light ":

> " Through such souls alone
> God stooping shows sufficient of His light
> For us in the dark to rise by."

As God, he confuses our perceptions of God's unity, bewilders our reason with endless contradictions, and turns away from the Supreme all those emotions of love and adoration which can only flow towards a single object, and which are the due of our Creator alone: as man, he gives us an example to strive after, a beacon to steer by; he is one more leader for humanity, one more star in our darkness. As God, all his words would be truth, and but few would enter into heaven, while hell would overflow with victims: as man, we may refuse to believe such a slander on our Father, and take all the comfort pledged to us by that name. Thank God, then, that Jesus is only man, human child of human parents: that we need not dwarf our conceptions of God to fit human faculties, or envelope the illimitable spirit in a baby's feeble frame. But though only man, he has reached a standard of human greatness which no other man, so far as we know, has touched: the very height of his character is almost a pledge of the truthfulness of the records in the main: his life had to be lived before its conception became possible, at that period and among such a people. They could recognise his greatness when it was before their eyes: they would scarcely have imagined it for themselves, more especially that, as we have seen, he was so different from the Jewish ideal. His code of morality stands unrivalled, and he was the first who taught the universal Fatherhood of God publicly and to the common people. Many of his loftiest precepts may be found in the books of the Rabbis, but it is the glorious prerogative of Jesus that he spread abroad among the many the wise and holy maxims that had hitherto been the sacred treasures of the few. With him none were too degraded to be called the children of the Father: none too simple to be worthy of the highest teaching. By example, as well as by precept, he taught that all men were brothers, and all the good he had he showered at their feet. "Pure in heart," he saw God, and what he saw he called all to see: he longed that all might share in his own joyous trust in the Father, and seemed to be always seeking for fresh images to describe the freedom and fulness of the universal love of God. In his unwavering love of truth, but his patience with doubters—in his personal purity, but his tenderness to the fallen—in his hatred of evil, but his friendliness to the sinner—we see splendid virtues rarely met in combination. His brotherliness, his yearning to raise the degraded, his lofty piety, his unswerving morality, his perfect self-sacrifice, are his indefeasible titles to human love and reverence. Of the world's benefactors he is the chief, not only by his own life, but by the enthusiasm he has known to inspire in others: "Our plummet has not sounded his depth:" words fail to tell what humanity owes to the Prophet of Nazareth. On his example the great Christian heroes have based their lives: from the foundation laid by his teaching the world is slowly rising to a purer faith in God. We need now such a leader as he was, one who would dare to follow the Father's will as he did, casting a long-prized revelation aside when it conflicts with the higher voice of conscience. It is the teaching of Jesus that Theism gladly makes its own, purifying it from the inconsistencies which mar its perfection. It is the example of Jesus which Theists are following, though they correct that example in some points by his loftiest sayings. It is the work of Jesus which Theists are carrying on, by worshipping, as he did, the Father, and the Father alone, and by endeavouring to turn all men's love, all men's hopes, and all men's adoration, to that "God and Father of all, who is above all, and through all, and," not in Jesus only, but "*in us all.*"

APPENDIX.

"Josephus mentions a Zacharias, son of Baruch ('Wars of the Jews,' Book iv., sec. 4), who was slain under the circumstances described by Jesus. His name would be more suitable at the close of the long list of Jewish crimes, as it occurred just before the destruction of Jerusalem. But, as it took place about thirty-four years after the death of Jesus, it is clear that he could not have referred to it; therefore, if we admit that he made no mistake, we strike a serious blow at the credibility of his historian, who then puts into his mouth a remark he never uttered."

Printed by Libri Plureos GmbH in Hamburg,
Germany